DHARAMSALA

DHARAMSALA

TIBETAN REFUGE

◆

Jeremy Russell

◆

Foreword by
His Holiness the Dalai Lama

Lustre Press
Roli Books

FOREWORD

Dharamsala has been my home for the greater part of my adult life since I left Tibet in 1959. I still remember well my first arrival here in the spring of 1960. We drove up by road from Pathankot station, through beautiful countryside, the lush green fields filled with trees and colourful flowers. After about an hour we caught our first glimpse of the gleaming white mountains of the Dhauladhar range towering in the distance. These peaks were also the first sight to greet my eyes when I awoke for the first time in my new home the following morning, and of course their presence remains the dominating feature of the landscape.

Dharamsala was where I was finally able to settle down after several years' pressure trying to deal with the Chinese occupation of my homeland, followed by the turmoil of my escape to India. Those early days were marked by a new kind of freedom, for although there was a lot of work to do ensuring the welfare of our ever increasing community of refugees, I finally had time and leisure to give more attention to my studies and my spiritual practice. In addition, I was physically freer and enjoyed walking and trekking into the nearby woods and hills. Dharamsala then was very much an abandoned British hill station, a quiet and sleepy backwater of the Punjab, not the bustling Himachali town that it is today. My mother shared those early years with me and it was here that she happily spent her final days.

During our stay here, we Tibetans have been able to construct several institutions that have served not only to enable us to preserve our identity and traditions, but also to share them with others. I believe that our schools and religious establishments, our government offices, the Institute for Performing Arts, the Library of Tibetan Works and Archives, the Tibetan Medical and Astrological Institute, the Norbulingka Institute and so forth vividly display Tibetans' resourcefulness and the richness and value of our ancient culture. This is one of the paradoxical benefits of our time in exile, for when Tibet was free few people from the outside world had access to it and our way of life was often shrouded in mystery and misunderstood.

One of the great personal pleasures of moving to my present residence in 1968 was that it gave me the opportunity to work in my garden, where I am able to plant trees and tend flowers with my own hands. However, this pleasure is also related to one of my few disappointments with life here. For much of the year, the summer and autumn especially, we enjoy a comfortable, pleasant climate, but this all changes in the humidity of monsoon. Dharamsala suffers from over-abundant rainfall, which, besides creating havoc in the garden, is causing increasingly severe damage to the local hillsides and the environment in general. It is then in particular that I miss the drier weather of Tibet.

Apart from this small reservation, I look back on my years so far in Dharamsala as happy ones. Having made me and my people warmly welcome since our first arrival, the people of Dharamsala have continued to show us remarkable kindness and affection over the years. Whatever the future may hold, and whenever our dreams of returning freely to our homeland are fulfilled, we will never forget our time in this delightful place that has served us as true refuge.

January 28, 1999

Page 1: Tibetan baby in a box.

Page 2: Monks chat on the temple verandah during a break in the course of teachings by the Dalai Lama.

Pages 4-5: The struggle for the restoration of freedom in Tibet goes on. Awareness of the Tibetan cause is spread by the sale of symbols such as these.

Page 6: The Dalai Lama in Dharamsala.

Page 9: His Holiness, the Dalai Lama, during the Long Life puja held in the Main Temple in McLeod Ganj in July 1994.

Pages 10-11: Monks from all over Dharamsala attending the inauguration of the Norbulinga Institute.

Introduction

✦

Dharamsala denotes a place of shelter for pilgrims, usually a hostel attached to one of the myriad temples that dot the Indian landscape. It is an apt name for the small hill town that is the headquarters of Kangra District in the north Indian state of Himachal Pradesh—for Dharamsala has functioned as a shelter of sorts right from the start and continues to do so today.

Following the British seizure of the Kangra fort and the annexation of Kangra district, Dharamsala was established as a hill station. It was host to sick soldiers and administrative officers and British wives and children escaping the heat of the plains in summer.

In 1947, many people left Dharamsala and moved to the newly created Pakistan, a relatively short journey away. At the same time, many travelled in the opposite direction, leaving their homes in Rawalpindi, Lahore and Peshawar, and arrived in Dharamsala. Many of them settled there and rebuilt their lives.

Barely thirteen years later, in 1960, His Holiness the Dalai Lama of Tibet was invited to take up temporary residence in Dharamsala, after his dramatic flight from his country following the Chinese communist takeover. He was accompanied by his family, his teachers and close advisors; eventually, a substantial lay and monastic Tibetan community followed him. He set up an administration of this new refugee community in Dharamsala that is, in effect, a government-in-exile.

At the beginning of the twenty-first century, Dharamsala is busy and thriving once more. Its population has expanded tremendously since the sleepy days before the Tibetans came, and building, both planned and unplanned, has proceeded apace. Besides becoming one of the most important towns of Himachal Pradesh, Dharamsala has become a major tourist destination. People flock not only from all over India, but from every corner of the globe to this quiet refuge. And yet, true to its historically cosmopolitan character, remarkable telecommunication facilities and a proliferation of Internet cafés, this shelter in the hills is no longer remote but in constant touch with the world at large.

Pages 12-13: The cool and peace of the wooded hills initially attracted the British to Dharamsala.

Pages 14-15: Dharamsala with the Dauladhar mountain range towering behind it.

Pages 16-17: Monks of Namgyal monastery constructing a sand mandala.

Historical Background

Dharamsala looks out over the beautiful Kangra valley, a region rich in ancient history. The kings of Kangra belonged to one of the oldest traceable genealogical lines in India. In the distant past the kingdom of Trigarta, and later the kingdom of Jalandhara, extended from the Dhauladhar mountains of the outer Himalayan range down to the plains. It was in this vicinity that Alexander the Great came to a final halt on the banks of the Beas river which runs from above Manali down through the Kangra valley until it reaches the plains. Aryan and Indian Pali inscriptions on a pair of boulders below Khanyara near Dharamsala dating to the end of the 1st century BCE (Before the Common Era or Before the Christian Era) suggest that there was a Buddhist monastery, the Krishna-yasasa Arama, nearby. Other archaeological evidence—Buddhist statues and so forth—suggest that the kingdom of Jalandhara was a centre of Hindu/Buddhist tantricism in the 7th century, when Buddhism was carried to Tibet. Chetru below Dharamsala is something of an archaeological mystery. Some assert that it has associations with the Pandava brothers, but there is also a suggestion that Chetru comes from the word *chaitya* or stupa, which may have stood at the confluence of two rivers. Further afield, the unique rock-cut temples at Masroor dedicated to Shiva, and the delightful temple compound at Baijnath are more than one thousand years old.

When the Muslim army of Mahmud of Ghazni entered India, it laid siege to the Kangra fort in 1009 CE and plundered the Kangra temple for its wealth. The temple at Jwalamukhi, where the deity is represented by flames emerging naturally from the ground, was admired by the Mughal emperor Akbar, who is alleged to have offered the gilded roof. Yet, today, visitors will be hard-pressed to find any sign that Muslims were ever there, their homes, places of worship and burial grounds seemingly forgotten.

Otherwise, what distinguishes Dharamsala from an ancient town like Kangra is not only its relative youth, but the fact that it has always been and

remains so cosmopolitan. The British founded it and attracted people to work for them. This polity included Sikhs and other Punjabis, people from Jammu and Gurkhas from Nepal. They came to live side by side with the indigenous people of the land, the Kangri people of the valley and the nomadic Gaddi tribes. Legend has it that four or five hundred years ago, the Gaddis migrated from Rajasthan, having lost their land there. They came to inhabit this region and the consequent Gaddi realm encompassed the Dhauladhar range from Kullu up to Chamba. These nomadic Hindu shepherds, as distinct from the Muslim Gujjar cattleherds elsewhere in Himachal Pradesh, take their flocks of sheep and goats over the high passes to seek mountain pastures in summer and the monsoon, but spend winter in the Kangra valley, where many own houses and land.

Pages 18-19: The Gaddi shepherds, indigenous to the hills around Dharamsala, lead their flocks over the high passes to richer pastures in summer and return to the Kangra valley in winter.

The British Era

The memorial to Lord Elgin, Viceroy of India, was erected by his widow after he died in Dharamsala. It stands beyond the head of the church.

Facing page: Mrs Nowrojee looks out from the entrance to the shop owned by her husband's family for nearly a century and a half.

Dharamsala was founded by the British who occupied the Kangra fort in 1846 and annexed the kingdom of Kangra. They then sought a cooler elevated position, from which they could overlook the Kangra valley, to garrison their forces. Thus, they established what is now the cantonment on the spur of the hills that has come to be known as Dharamsala. The army camp continues to have a commanding view of the valley.

Earlier the kings of Kangra had also occupied these hills for much the same reasons. Accounts of the origin of the name Dharamsala vary—one tells that Dharam Chand, a king, built some kind of a fort on Dharamkot hill, another secure vantage point. He also apparently erected a *dharamsala*, a place for people to rest, while waiting for an audience with him.

In due course, with the British army settled on the ridge, civilian residences came up in the woods above. The initial temporary camp at Dharamsala was upgraded into a cantonment in 1849. At the same time, the local Divisional Commissioner, John Lawrence, later Commissioner for the Punjab and Viceroy, built one of the first civilian houses. Eventually the cantonment attracted to it settlements which later became the villages of McLeod Ganj and Forsyth Ganj, where people who served the army as cooks, cleaners, tailors, and so forth, lived. The building of the Church of St. John in the Wilderness in 1852 is indicative of how settled the community became in a relatively short time. Villas occupied by officials such as the Deputy Commissioner and the Forest Officer came up in the forest above McLeod Ganj. It was as if the hillside had been laid out in order of social status. The civilian officers had villas up on the hill; the military were a little further down and the offices of the civil administration were below them.

One of Dharamsala's most enduring landmarks is Mr Nowrojee's shop which dates back to about 1860. The fact that this thriving Parsee businessman from Lahore saw fit to establish a branch in the hills is evidence that there was a sufficiently large community to be served by such an enterprising provisioner.

Lord Elgin of Kincardine was Viceroy of India from 1860 to 1863. He developed a particular fondness for Dharamsala and it was probably this affection that gave rise to the legend that Dharamsala was to become the summer capital of British India. In any event he did not live to fulfill this wish, for he died in Dharamsala in 1863. His widow endowed an elaborate memorial to him that stands beyond the head of the church, and a pair of stained-glass windows, attributed to Edwin Byrne-Jones (1833-1898), English painter, designer and illustrator who was a member of the pre-Raphaelite movement.

The inscription reads: Hari Om Mani Padme Hum— *Hail to the Jewel in the Lotus.*

Facing page: Woman prays on lingor *path around the palace of His Holiness the Dalai Lama.*

The British community continued to thrive, attracting all kinds of people including sick soldiers and wives of officers and missionaries, who treated Dharamsala as a place of rest. Consequently, it developed into a classic hill station, which with Dalhousie, would have served Lahore as much as Delhi and the rest of the huge pre-partition Punjab. Even today, if you walk westwards out of McLeod Ganj, you can imagine the *pukka sahibs* riding the narrow roads and myriad cobbled paths to the church on Sundays and perhaps on to Mr Nowrojee's shop to pick up something to while away the afternoon.

Having come up as a British settlement, Dharamsala took a major blow on April 4, 1905, when a huge earthquake struck it early in the morning with devastating force. Eyewitness accounts relate that all the buildings in the Kangra area were either demolished or rendered uninhabitable. The church was one of the very few buildings to survive, but most of the residential areas of Kangra and Dharamsala had to be rebuilt. In this process, a major relocation took place, giving rise to the upper, middle and lower areas of the town. With the reconstruction, the courts, police station and lock-up, as well as offices of the various administrative departments were re-established in lower Dharamsala, where they still stand today. The market was reconstructed at what is now Kotwali Bazaar. Inevitably, the villas and bungalows of the hill station proper came up again in the forests above McLeod Ganj and Forsyth Ganj, for only there at 6000 feet above sea level was there any real refuge from the summer heat.

Life in Dharamsala saw gradual improvements such as the construction of the hydroelectric powerhouse at Jogindernagar, which brought electricity to the hill station in the late 1920s, and the introduction of the Kangra Valley narrow-gauge railway. At the same time, the Nowrojees introduced the first two cars that ran up to Dharamsala from the railhead at Pathankot. Even now, older residents remember how Dharamsala used to be supplied from Pathankot by bullock and camel cart.

With Indian independence approaching in 1947, many of the British planned to stay on. However, the horrors that accompanied the unfortunate partition of the country put paid to their dreams. Dharamsala, the tranquil and slightly remote hill station, suddenly found itself relatively close to the newly wrought border. One of the effects was a substantial migration of people to Pakistan. Some people say that 70 per cent of the people in Kotwali Bazaar left in the late summer of 1947. In turn many families arrived from Peshawar, Rawalpindi, Lahore and those regions of Punjab and the North West Frontier that had ended up as Pakistan. With the dreadful carnage that took place in this great upheaval, many Britishers, who had thought they would make a go of it in the *new* India, took fright, fled and never returned. The upper reaches of Dharamsala, where the British and European population used to live, was largely abandoned. The bungalows and villas were left behind in the care of Mr Nowrojee, who, amongst so many other things, was the local estate agent.

Over the next twelve or thirteen years, upper Dharamsala became quite dilapidated. In 1960, the newly exiled Dalai Lama was invited to settle in Dharamsala rather than in Mussoorie, where he had been provided initial sanctuary. It seems that he and the refugees following him received an especially sympathetic reception from the population of Dharamsala, many of whom had not long before been refugees themselves. The latter knew what it was like to lose the land they had grown up in and to have to rebuild their lives elsewhere. With the arrival of the Dalai Lama and the Tibetans who gathered around him, Dharamsala gained a new lease of life.

What remains today of the British era are a few bungalows and villas which have since been occupied by Tibetans and have acquired other associations. Swarg Ashram, for example, the house where the Dalai Lama first lived in Dharamsala, is now the Mountaineering Institute. The house a

The bell of the Church of St. John in the Wilderness was broken in the earthquake in 1905. Though a new bell was cast in London and carried to India, it was never raised to the tower again.

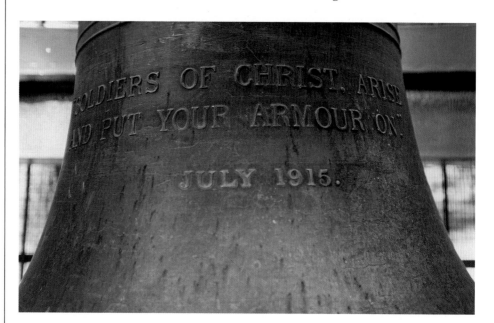

little further up the hill where his junior tutor, Trijang Rinpoche, first lived, now functions as the Tushita Meditation Centre. Dharamsala cantonment, like other cantonments the length and breadth of India, is home to regiments of the Indian army. Due to its mild climate and pleasant environment, Dharamsala continues to be regarded as an enviable posting by army officials.

Mr Nowrojee's shop, which provided for the British community from 1860 until 1947, still does thriving business and is filled with mementos of those bygone times. It offers priceless candy jars, rare advertising cards, placards, fixtures and fittings dating from a period of greater prosperity and which are older than most of the people visiting the shop. The Nowrojees were innovators in many ways: apart from being provision merchants and newsagents, they ran an aerated water plant, provided the only local taxi service and functioned as auctioneers and estate agents. The present Mr Nowrojee, who is now in his eighties, is one of the few people to have witnessed the entire ebb and flow of Dharamsala's history.

The Church of St. John in the Wilderness

✟

Known as the 'army church', the Church of St. John in the Wilderness was built in 1852 to meet the needs of the British soldiers posted at Dharamsala. Standing alone amidst the towering deodar (Himalayan cedar) trees, it might be mistaken for a quiet kirk (church) somewhere in Scotland. This sturdy stone building, well constructed of hand-dressed local granite, withstood the 1905 earthquake, although pieces of the broken front scattered here and there are evidence that it suffered significant damage. There used to be a steeple, and presumably a bell, which apparently fell at that time. A new bell was cast in London, surprisingly in 1915 when Europe was embroiled in war. And, although we can imagine its long and careful journey by sea, probably to Bombay, then by rail to Pathankot and from there to the church by bullock cart, it was never raised into the tower again, but remained hung from beams resting between supporting walls in the garden outside. This support was rebuilt in 1995 and inaugurated by the Duke of Gloucester who was fortuitously visiting Dharamsala at the time. When thieves attempted to steal this bell in the spring of 1998, they fortunately dropped it, relatively unharmed, a couple of hundred yards up the road.

A new arrival in Dharamsala awaits an audience with the Dalai Lama.

In the church itself there are plaques mostly commemorating military men who have died, but rarely in action. There is a famous one for the man who died in a fight with a bear and another above the organ, put up by a girl for her poor young fiancée who died on the eve of their wedding. In the graveyard are buried people who died in Dharamsala, presumably of ailments like dysentery and diarrhoea that we would not expect to be fatal these days. A century and a half ago, there were no antibiotics and probably an insufficient supply of clean water. There are many graves of small children. It is also touching how many of the gravestones were put up by fellow officers and soldiers as a mark of affection and esteem.

Mother of Ngawarg Gyaltzen, a musicologist trained in Dharamsala and USA, and who has been imprisoned by the Chinese for 18 years in Tibet.

The Arrival of the Tibetans

✟

With the coming of the Tibetans, upper Dharamsala began to stir once more. For the first decade—throughout the sixties—life must have been very difficult for the refugees. Most of them worked at building roads and lived in makeshift camps. They were traumatised—having fled their homes and having lost their country to the invading Chinese. They lived in great expectation that they would return soon, that the dispute with China would be settled swiftly. In retrospect, those years were a transitional period

Families just arrived from Tibet await their fate.

Father and daughter are united after many years when he is able to leave Tibet at last.

as the exiled Tibetan community came to terms with what had happened. Even in the early seventies most Tibetans were still living in makeshift houses put together from fruit and vegetable boxes with flattened oil tins for roofing.

However, the Dalai Lama lost no time in assembling a secretariat which would function both as a government-in-exile and administer the refugee community. He received a great deal of backing and encouragement from the then Indian Prime Minister Jawaharlal Nehru. Many Tibetans in those early years expected that they would receive support to fight the Chinese and somehow reclaim their country. However, what Nehru counselled the Dalai Lama to do if he wished to save his culture and his nation, was to ensure the education of Tibetan children. He was convinced that that was the way to secure Tibet's future.

Thekchen Chöling—the Tsuglagkhang and the Dalai Lama's Palace

✠

In the early years of the Tibetan settlement in Dharamsala, the Dalai Lama was accommodated in a house known as Swarg Ashram, which sits on extensive grounds on the road climbing into the woods above McLeod Ganj.

At that time his two tutors also occupied houses on the same hill: Trijang Rinpoche lived in the house which is now the Tushita Meditation Centre and the senior tutor, Ling Rinpoche, lived a little higher up in Chopra House. This is where the Tibetan administration was initially centred.

In the course of time, various religious bodies were attracted to His Holiness's presence. For example, the Namgyal Monastery, the Dalai Lama's personal monastery, which had been temporarily established in Dalhousie in the mid 60s, moved to Dharamsala. In the early years of exile few Tibetans thought that they were going to be in exile for a long time. Initially they made little effort to re-establish their institutions such as temples and others. But after nearly ten years, there was an urge to build the present Tsuglagkhang or main temple at Thekchen Chöling on the crest of the ridge which McLeod Ganj bestrides.

However, mindful of the refugee community's limited budget, the Dalai Lama made it clear that the need was not to build a lavish temple as they would have done in Tibet. What was required was a simple, functional building which would allow people to gather to observe their religious ceremonies and practices. This is why the temple is a plain and square concrete structure. Nevertheless, the original building has continued to be extended and improved upon.

On entering the temple, as everyone is welcome to do even when there are religious functions taking place, the visitor's first encounter is with a large statue of Buddha Shakyamuni, the historical Buddha. Seated in saffron robes in a posture of meditation, his right hand touches the ground, calling

When mothers are at work, their babies stay here.

Life in exile offers some freedom from fear.

Pages 28-29: His Holiness the Fourteenth Dalai Lama—Dharamsala's most revered resident.

Pages 30-31: Long-life ceremony for the Dalai Lama in the Tsnglagkhang—the main temple.

the earth to witness his awakening to enlightenment. His left hand rests in his lap, holding the alms bowl of a monk. This statue of the Buddha is the major focus of the temple. As people enter, they pay their respects, often by bowing down three times and touching their heads to the ground in prostration, as a mark of admiration and aspiration of attaining the state of enlightenment themselves.

On either side of the statue are cupboards from floor to ceiling, containing the volumes of the two major collections of Tibetan Buddhist scriptures: the *Kangyur*—the translated words of the Buddha and the *Tengyur*—the collection of translated commentaries of later Buddhist teachers. These books are long and narrow, emulating the original palm-leaf manuscripts of ancient India. They are placed lengthways in the cabinet so that only the ornate tags bearing their titles can be seen.

On the eastern wall, next to the door, hangs a large painting depicting the three religious kings of Tibet: Songtsen Gampo (born 605 CE), Trisong Detsen (born 742 CE) and Ralpachen (died 848 CE), who are honoured for having initiated the introduction of Buddhism into Tibet. During the reign of

Pages 32-33: His Holiness the Dalai Lama participates in prayers in the Tsnglagkhang. Behind him is the statue of Shakyamuni, the historical Buddha. The statue is flanked by cupboards containing the scriptures. To the right of the Dalai Lama are statues of Padmasambhava or Guru Rimpoche and a thousand armed Avalokiteshvara.

King Songtsen Gampo, Tibet had become a major military power in Asia, its influence extending well into western China, up to Mongolia, down to the banks of the Ganges, and even westwards towards Swat in what is now Pakistan. It is almost as if Songtsen Gampo realised that the country had reached its peak in one aspect of its development and, in order to lead the nation in a new direction, had set about introducing Buddhist culture, primarily from India.

This entailed developing a written language. Taking a Sanskrit model, a written language and grammar were composed by one of the king's ministers, Thonmi Sambhota, who had been sent to Kashmir for this purpose. A huge project was then begun to translate the existing Sanskrit literature into Tibetan and literally create a body of literature which emulated and simulated Indian Buddhist culture. This enterprise continued under the auspices of the other two religious kings.

Amongst King Songtsen Gampo's several wives, Princess Brikuti from Nepal and Princess Wengchen from China encouraged his awareness of Buddhism. Under their influence the Lhasa Tsuglagkhang or Jokhang and

Ramoche temples were constructed. During the reign of King Trisong Detsen a century later, Buddhism was formally declared the state religion and Tibet's first Buddhist institutions were established. The great Indian abbot Shantarakshita ordained the first seven Tibetan monks and tried to found a monastery. But, so the story goes, Tibet's local spirits were opposed to his activities, and whatever was built during the day was demolished at night.

Shantarakshita informed the king that he did not have sufficient influence to achieve what was required and recommended that he invite the great charismatic adept, Padmasambhava, the Lotus Born Guru, from India, which Trisong Detsen duly did. Padmasambhava visited Tibet, pacified the interfering forces, and, with Shantarakshita, established the great monastery of Samye (767 CE) and many other religious establishments. Both these important figures are depicted in the painting, in the space above and behind the three kings.

Padmasambhava or Guru Rinpoche, the Precious Guru as he is popularly known, is also portrayed in the large fierce-looking statue seated in the alcove on the western side of the temple. He is regarded by many Tibetans with a respect and gratitude second only to that accorded the historical Buddha, because he actually established Buddhism in Tibet.

To the left of the statue of Padmasambhava is a large standing statue with eleven heads and a thousand arms, each of which has an eye in the palm of the hand. This is a representation of Avalokitesvara or Chenresig—the Bodhisattva of compassion, who is as close as is possible to being the patron deity of Tibet. It is his six-syllable mantra, *Om Manipadme Hung*, which is on the lips of so many Tibetans as they go about their lives. Moreover, the Dalai Lamas are traditionally regarded as human emanations of Avalokitesvara, so there is clearly a very strong link between this deity and Tibet.

At the feet of the Avalokitesvara statue there is a small glass-fronted cabinet containing some broken stone heads which belonged to a very

Pages 36-37: Monks of Namgyal Monastery blow long horns while members of the Tibetan Government-in-Exile look on during the New Year rooftop ceremonies.

similar statue that used to stand in the Jokhang in Lhasa. It was destroyed in 1967 during the cultural revolution and these fragments were salvaged and brought to India. They were presented to the Dalai Lama, who placed them here.

To the left of the Avalokitesvara is a small statue of Dipankara Atisha, the great Indian Buddhist teacher from the monastery of Vikramashila, who was invited to Tibet in 1042. By this time the initial wave of Buddhist culture had become somewhat diffused and confused. Dipankara Atisha brought a new clarity to Tibetan Buddhism, emphasising the need for the monastic community to be pure. He also established the renowned genre of Buddhist literature that is known as the *Stages of the Path of Enlightenment*. In this he laid out, in an easily comprehensible form, the stages of spiritual practice from the simplest aspiration for freedom from anguished rebirth to liberation, to final enlightenment for the sake of all sentient beings.

Placed before this set of statues are offerings of bowls of clean water and butter lamps, typical of Tibetan Buddhist temples. The golden lamps before the Avalokitesvara and Padmasambhava statues are offered particularly when people wish to pray for the sick and the recently dead.

Hanging on the walls of the temple are *thangkas*, the scroll paintings which often depict stories from the Buddha's life or illustrate meditational, or long-life, tutelary deities. These are painted on cloth and mounted on lavish silk brocade. Many Tibetans lived a nomadic existence and these paintings could be rolled up and carried with them when they set off for the next pasture.

Behind the temple are the kitchens where enormous cauldrons—five or six feet across—are heated over wood fires to boil huge amounts of tea when

there are large gatherings in the temple. There are occasions when two or three thousand monks and nuns and, perhaps, as many lay people assemble to listen to the Dalai Lama's public teachings as part of the Great Prayer Festival in spring.

Besides being a location for public teaching, the temple is a place where people come to offer personal prayers. They also come to make offerings before the Dalai Lama's throne, a throne that is erected out of respect for religious teaching. In fact, when the Dalai Lama himself comes to sit on that throne in order to teach, he first bows before it. This is a throne on which only he can sit and, as such, paying respect to the throne is like paying respect to him. The temple is also a site for the public and the monastic communities of the locality to gather to say prayers, which they do at various times throughout the year. Sometimes they gather for week-long sessions during which they recite 100,000 prayers or offerings and a great number of mantras. Outside, individuals can often be seen performing prostrations and they too may have a target of 100,000.

His Holiness the Dalai Lama presides over the rooftop ceremonies at the Tibetan New Year, wherein offerings are made to Palden Lhamo (Sri Devi).

The Namgyal Monastery

Adjacent to the main temple are the buildings of the Namgyal Monastery, which has a special function in the Tibetan Buddhist structure because of its long association with the Dalai Lamas. This began with the third Dalai Lama, Sonam Gyatso, when he was accepted as spiritual mentor of the Mongol chieftain Gushri Khan, from whom he received the title 'Dalai Lama' in tribute to his oceanic qualities. He gathered some monks together to say

The New Temple in the Namgyal Monastery. Thangkas *and deities being consecrated during Buddha's descent from Tushita (heavenly realms).*

regular prayers for the long life of Gushri Khan and this group seems eventually to have evolved into the Namgyal Monastery.

When the Fifth Dalai Lama became the overall ruler of a united Tibet and established himself in the Potala Palace, which he had built on the Red Hill in Lhasa, the Namgyal Monastery was accommodated in the red West Wing. The monastery came to have great significance in the Ganden Podrang government founded by the Fifth Dalai Lama. This unique spiritual and temporal form of government consisted of both monastic and lay officials, 175 of each, and to echo these numbers, there were 175 monks in the Namgyal Monastery.

Tibetan women churning salt, butter and tea leaves in a traditional domo.

Their function was to perform rituals and prayers for the benefit of Tibet and to support the Dalai Lama in his religious activities. To this day the Dalai Lama's personal attendants are drawn from amongst the monks of the Namgyal Monastery. They support him when he is expounding Buddhist teachings and performing ceremonies such as tantric initiations. When he grants the Kalachakra initiation, which he gives to large groups of people, he is supported by a team of about 18 monks from the Namgyal Monastery. They are skilled in the arts of creating sand *mandalas*, performing the dances, manufacturing the requisite ritual cakes, and so forth.

Offerings of candles for the Long Life puja of the Dalai Lama.

Of the 175 monks belonging to the monastery in Tibet, about 30 managed to escape into exile. Of these, half survived and were able to train a new body of monks when the monastery was re-established in Dharamsala. They have passed on nearly all the ritual traditions of the Namgyal Monastery. However, the Dalai Lama is particularly concerned that there should no longer be such a proliferation of monasteries whose only function is to perform rituals, as there was sometimes in Tibet. He feels it is important that monks should have sufficient education to understand what they are doing in the rituals and to understand the context in which they function. The monks of Namgyal Monastery, like the monks of Nechung Monastery, have added to their curriculum of ritual studies, studies of Buddhist philosophy and the practice of debate, in addition to a certain amount of modern education. They now have a much broader command of their ancient Buddhist culture than perhaps their predecessors would have had in Tibet.

For many years, the Namgyal Monastery used the Tsuglagkhang temple as the site for many of the rituals which they perform in a cycle, a calendar of events throughout the year. Ultimately a need emerged for another location, so they constructed alongside the main temple what has come to be known as the Kalachakra temple. This is mainly because the paintings on its walls were dominated by depictions of the Kalachakra *mandala*. Now the monastery is able to continue their cycle of practices, even when the main temple is in use for other purposes.

The paintings on the three walls at the head of the temple illustrate the Namgyal Monastery's spiritual inheritance. On either side are the body and mind *mandalas* of the meditational deity Kalachakra, representing his celestial mansion and entourage of meditational deities.

The paintings inside this temple are particularly fine examples of Tibetan Buddhist artwork. The artists here have emulated the technique used for painting *thangkas*. A canvas was attached to the wall and teams of painters worked for 18 months on scaffolding to complete the project.

Thekchen Chöling is the focus of the Tibetan New Year celebrations, which generally take place in February or March. First, there are ceremonies to dispose of the symbols of the old year and any residual negativity to be able to begin the new year afresh. The new year dawns with a ceremony on the temple roof presided over by the Dalai Lama. This consists of solemn prayers to Palden Lhamo (Sri Devi), one of the state guardians of Tibet. Two weeks later, on the fifteenth of the first Tibetan month, the full moon day, the traditional Great Prayer Festival begins with the Dalai Lama reading one of the stories of the births of the Buddha prior to his life as the historical Buddha. This is followed by what has come to be known as the Spring Teachings—two weeks in which the Dalai Lama gives religious discourses to the public. This used to take place in the temple itself with the Dalai Lama sitting on the throne, surrounded by monks and nuns, and the lay people behind them, spilling out on to the verandahs and walkways. In the

mid-nineties, the Dalai Lama decided that it is more convenient for everyone to gather in the temple garden.

At the far end from the temple in the garden is the gate to the Dalai Lama's personal residential compound. The first set of buildings beyond the gate contain his private office, audience chambers, and so forth. His personal residence stands in the garden, just over the peak of the hill. The audience chambers are where he meets individuals for personal or private interviews and where he receives large groups who come to take his blessings. He makes a point of meeting everybody who reaches Dharamsala from Tibet.

Institute of Buddhist Dialectics

Behind and below the temple is the Institute of Buddhist Dialectics, an ecumenical school of monks who train in the tradition of dialectics followed in the great monastic institutions of Tibet. Formal debate or dialectics is a means by which logic can be applied to the meaning of the scriptures, ensuring that a correct and affirmed understanding can be maintained. Traditionally monks memorise the text they are studying—often the translation of an Indian Buddhist text. After that they receive an oral explanation of the text and then debate their understanding with their fellow students.

Customarily, one monk stands and, with elaborate gestures, poses a challenging question to his colleague seated on the ground who, in turn, seeks to answer. This is not merely an intellectual, but also a highly physical exercise involving the clapping of hands, the stamping of feet and the swinging of rosaries, which symbolise driving out misunderstandings and awakening

beings from the sleep of ignorance. The process stimulates a sharpness of intellect and a very deep and thorough understanding of the material studied. Most days, during the late afternoon, visitors to Thekchen Chöling may find monks from the Institute of Buddhist Dialectics or from the Namgyal Monastery in the temple garden practising this skill. It is a great spectacle.

The Mani Path

Running around the crest of the ridge, on which the temple and the Dalai Lama's residence stand, is a path popularly known as the Lingkhor, the circumambulatory path or the Mani Path. Like many circumambulatory routes in Tibet, it is lined by heaps of stones marked with the six-syllable mantra *Om Manipadme Hung*. People take a turn around the hill particularly during the early morning and evening, combining the benefits of a brisk walk with the spiritual potential of paying respect to religious objects. At a couple of places next to the path you will come across a tent sheltering a man carving *mani* stones, which the devout buy from him to place on one of the cairns. Below the path, an old people's home for retired members of the Tibetan administration has recently been established.

Shrines of the three protective deities of Tibet. The prayer flags behind hang over the Lingkhor or the Mani Path (the circumambulatory path).

Facing page: An early morning devotee turns one of the giant prayer wheels as he circumambulates the Mani Path.

At the southernmost point the path opens out into a great yard where, particularly on Wednesdays when the Dalai Lama is out of town, Tibetans offer incense and hoist prayer flags to Tibet's protective deities to ensure his welfare. These pieces of coloured cloth have been imprinted with prayers or sections of scripture carved on wood blocks, whose spirit is then carried over the land by the wind.

The Parliament-in-Exile during a session. The parliament supervises the running of the various departments of administration.

Facing page: An accomplished nun often consulted for divination about the future and other issues.

Gangchen Kyishong: The Tibetan Government-in-Exile

Further down the hill is the compound known as Gangchen Kyishong, the seat of the Tibetan government-in-exile. This is where the Assembly of Tibetan People's Deputies, the elected parliament-in-exile oversees the running of the various departments of the administration including the Departments of Religion and Culture, Home, Education, Health, Finance, Information and International Relations. These various departments have a dual function of contributing to the struggle for freedom in Tibet, besides administering to the needs of the Tibetan refugee community.

The Tibetan Library

Above: The Tibetan library has a highly decorative verandah with brightly painted pillars and capitals.

Below: Statue of Arya Tara.

Facing page: Tibetans circumambulate the Library early morning and evening, thinking good thoughts. The Library is also regarded as a holy place.

One of the earliest buildings in Gangchen Kyishong is the Library of Tibetan Works and Archives. Established in 1971, it is the cultural repository of the community-in-exile. When the Dalai Lama left Tibet in 1959, many of the people who followed him carried little more than what they stood up in. However, during the ensuing decade, people continued to leave Tibet and, recognising the threat that the Chinese presence in Tibet posed to Tibetan culture, they brought statues, paintings and books with them, many of them salvaged from destroyed monasteries and temples. These they would bring to Dharamsala to offer to the Dalai Lama. By the end of the sixties, the Dalai Lama recognised the need for an institution to preserve this unique collection of Tibetan artefacts and founded the Library of Tibetan Works and Archives in 1971.

When it was built, the Tibetan Library, as it is fondly known, was the only Tibetan-style building in Dharamsala, which made it something of a cultural asset by itself. It was modelled on an aristocratic house which used to stand in Lhasa and has such typical features as the broad base with whitewashed walls which taper inwards as the building rises. The deep windows have the broad black border known as a beard; the protruding sill above, and a red frieze which runs around the top of the walls. But what immediately catches the eye is the highly decorative verandah with its brightly painted pillars and capitals in front of the grand red doors with their tassled brass knobs.

Books occupy the entire ground floor. These include 70,000 Tibetan books and documents brought out of Tibet and about 10,000 books in English and foreign languages dealing with Buddhism and Tibet-related affairs.

Tibetan literature has its origins in the great translating enterprise which began in the 7th and 8th centuries. It continued through to the 13th century in an ongoing process of refinement and editing until the scriptures had been gathered in two main collections: the *Kangyur,* or translations of the actual words of the Buddha, and the *Tengyur,* the supplementary commentaries of later Buddhist teachers. When they embarked on this great project, Tibetans took great pains to emulate Indian literature in every respect. They even followed the physical pattern of the books, writing them on long strips of paper which resembled the palm leaves of ancient Indian scriptures. In the centre of these pages two circles would be drawn indicating the position where a cord was threaded through the pages of Indian books to bind them together. Despite wrapping their books in cloth, for several hundred years Tibetans continued to draw circles on their pages in deference to the Indian tradition.

Initially, books in Tibet were handwritten, using a mixture of stove black for ink on a very strong but light paper made from a Tibetan grass.

The Nechung Monastery in Dharamsala is the seat of the State Oracle.

Both, copying out scriptures and sponsoring their production, were regarded as acts of piety. In due course, books became more elaborate—like the illustrated manuscripts of medieval Europe. They included illustrated title pages bearing the title in Sanskrit and its translation into Tibetan, featuring intricate, coloured paintings, often related to the Buddha. Subsequent pages might also be written in alternating lines of gold and silver on a blue background.

With the introduction of block printing from China, the scriptures could be reproduced as standard editions. But even this method required a huge investment of skilled labour. Every folio was represented by a single wood block with the front page on one side and the back on the other. The words were written in reverse on the wood and then carefully carved out. Printing was done entirely by hand, so block printing did not suddenly lead to mass production. But it did allow for the production of exact copies. Previously, if a monastery had wanted to acquire a particular book or collection of books, it would have borrowed an existing version from another monastery and made a handwritten copy. Inevitably, in the course of writing by hand, some earlier mistakes might have been corrected, but

others would have been introduced, giving rise continually to variant editions.

In the 13th and 14th centuries CE, an indigenous Tibetan literature began to emerge. Teachers and scholars had assimilated Buddhist culture sufficiently and had the confidence to write their own books. Consequently, besides the *Kangyur* and *Tengyur*, the two collections of scriptures translated largely from Indian sources, Tibetan literature expanded with the collected works of particular teachers. The manuscript room of the Tibetan Library contains several editions of the *Kangyur*, a couple of editions of the *Tengyur* and many collections of works brought out of Tibet which were written by illustrious lamas. This is one of the most precious collections of Tibetan books anywhere in the world.

Upstairs, in the centre of the building, a large hall contains the museum which is home to several hundred typically Tibetan Buddhist statues. Most households in Tibet would have had some form of household altar containing a statue of the Buddha or some other religious figure. In these cabinets are statues of the historical Buddha and Bodhisattvas or meditational deities who embody particular qualities: one such example is

Ex-prisoners of the Chinese in Tibet, these Tibetans now find useful employment in exile by working in a bakery.

Pages 56-57: A ritual at Nechung Monastery, led by the medium of the State Oracle.

*Prayers and offerings at a Long
Life ceremony being performed at
the Kalachakra Temple.*

that of Manjushri who wields the sword of wisdom which cuts through ignorance. These figures are distinguished by their characteristics, by the hand gestures and the implements that they carry, which represent qualities to which a spiritual practitioner might aspire. The latter may either address prayers to, or meditate on such a figure, visualising the figure in front of himself or visualising himself as one of these forms. These statues are not mere works of art, but religious objects. They are hollow and must be filled with rolls of scriptures and other substances such as incense before they are regarded as properly complete. The faces are painted, often with gold, by artists whose final task is to open—that is to paint in—their eyes. They are consecrated by monks who say prayers over or before them.

The museum also possesses a fine collection of *thangkas*. Some of these are packed with detail, particularly when they depict stories of the life of the Buddha or other spiritual teachers. Others function more as supports for meditational practice, portraying the meditational deity that the meditator visualises in his or her practice. Typically this *thangka* is hung in front of or in view of the meditator's seat. *Thangka* paintings may also be commissioned when there is a need to generate spiritual merit, for example, when a relative or friend has died.

Unique to this museum are two quite different examples of three-dimensional *mandalas*. One is carved of wood and represents the celestial residence of the deity of compassion, Avalokiteshvara. It has all the qualities of an ideal residence. Like the two-dimensional *thangka* painting, it serves to stimulate a meditator's imagination. The second *mandala* belongs to Arya Tara, the female embodiment of the Buddha's virtuous activity. It is created in the unusual medium known as thread cross, in which the planes consist of coloured threads wound on a light frame.

Besides its rich collection of religious objects, the museum also exhibits a collection of tea bowls, some of them porcelain, on elaborate stands with the requisite lid to keep the tea warm. Tea was the staple drink of Tibet. It is said that you could travel the length and breadth of the country carrying only a bag of *tsampa*, roasted barley flour, and your tea bowl. That would be sufficient, because you would be offered tea wherever you were.

The Tibetan Library is the focus of several other activities including classes by qualified lamas on Buddhist philosophy, from Tibetan texts translated into English. These classes have continued since the very foundation of the Library in 1971 and have been attended by hundreds of people from all over the world.

An ongoing project involves making audio recordings of the stories and recollections of a wide cross-section of the Tibetan society who can remember life in old Tibet. A team of old gentlemen well qualified to write Tibetan are steadily transcribing many of these reminiscences so that they may eventually be published. Elsewhere in the complex, work goes on: translating Tibetan books into English, teaching Tibetan language and preparing material for publication.

Nechung Monastery

✝

Another ritual being performed at the Nechung Monastery. This ceremony is also led by the State Oracle.

Below the Library of Tibetan Works and Archives, but still within the compound of the Tibetan government-in-exile, stands Nechung, the small monastery of the state oracle. There has been a close connection between this oracle and its presiding, protective spirit going back to the Great Fifth Dalai Lama, the first person to have governed a unified Tibet since the disintegration of the original Tibetan empire in the 8th-9th centuries. The state oracle's responsibility is to advise the Tibetan government and ensure its welfare. The temple at Nechung has been constructed with great care in the traditional manner but with modern materials. Visitors are very likely to find one of the cycle of rituals performed by the monks throughout the year going on here, to the strident accompaniment of horns, drums and cymbals.

Over the last thirty years Dharamsala has attracted people from the world over with an interest in Tibetan Buddhism and Tibetan culture. Many have attended classes at the Library of Tibetan Works and Archives and studied traditional Buddhist culture as it was preserved in Tibet. Some who have wished to put this experience into practice in actual meditation have participated in courses at the Tushita Meditation Centre which is perched above McLeod Ganj on the road to Triond. Presently there are facilities for individual meditators to go into retreat, and opportunities for people to attend group retreats with access to advice from experienced meditators.

The Tibetan Medical Centre (Men-tsee-khang)

The Tibetan Medical and Astrological Centre was established in exile to preserve the traditions that had been the responsibility of the Medical College on Chagpori hill in Lhasa since it was founded by *Desi* Sangye Gyatso, the regent of the Fifth Dalai Lama in the seventeenth century. The Men-tsee-khang continues to train doctors, pharmacists and astrologers, besides producing traditional Tibetan medicine, calendars, horoscopes, and so forth. The public can attend the clinic: a doctor examines the pulse in the patient's wrist and perhaps a sample of the first urine of the day. From this he or she can diagnose the patient's condition and prescribe various medicines, dietary advice such as avoiding oily food, and behavioural recommendations such as keeping the stomach warm or drinking hot rather than cold water.

The Tibetan medical system is very effective in treating digestive and nervous disorders and remarkably effective in dealing with hepatitis and other liver ailments. The Tibetan medical system can often help where Western medicine has little to offer. Whereas a Western doctor may tell you to come back in a week if you feel no better, a Tibetan physician can immediately pinpoint what is wrong and give you something to restore the balance of your health.

The astrological department can be approached to cast a horoscope, although this may require more faith than Tibetan medicine does. This department is also responsible for drawing up the popular Tibetan calendar annually. Following a lunar system as it does, it requires recalculation every year. Since months do not necessarily consist of a regular number of days, the astrological department has to calculate when some dates will be repeated and others will be missing. For example, for reasons of auspiciousness, the nineteenth may occur twice in one month, but the twelfth may be missing from another.

The Men-tsee-khang also incorporates the largest Tibetan pharmacy outside Tibet; it has been partly automated with equipment supplied from Germany. At certain times of the year, the staff goes up into the hills around Dharamsala, as well as around Lahaul and Manali, to gather leaves, flowers and other parts of plants to be made into medicines. In the recently opened museum, the medical *tantras,* which are the fundamental texts of this medical system, are vividly displayed as *thangkas.* Another interesting painting shows the process of conception, gestation and birth. Two cabinets contain all the texts that someone studying as a doctor or as an astrologer must master. There are also fascinating displays of the various mineral and herbal substances that go into the making of the medicines.

Traditional Tibetan Physicians

McLeod Ganj is host to a number of Tibetan doctors. Dr Yeshe Dhonden, for example, is definitely one of the more-famous personalities of McLeod Ganj. He trained at Lhasa's principal medical college on Chakpori Hill with one of the great physicians of the early part of the century. In exile he served as personal physician to the Dalai Lama and continues to practice in Dharamsala where he is consulted by people interested in Tibetan medicine. He can look you in the eye, take your pulse, examine a specimen of your urine and give you an account of the present state of your health and of past ailments reaching back into your childhood. Not only can he recognise what is wrong with you, but he also prescribes gentle remedies to set you right.

McLeod Ganj - The Namgyal Stupa

As you walk through the village of McLeod Ganj, the most prominent landmark is the Namgyal stupa or *chorten*, a typical Buddhist reliquary monument standing in the middle of the main street. Monuments like this are to be found wherever Buddhism has spread, providing a focus for the physical aspect of spiritual practice. People bow down before the stupa and circumambulate it. In the early days, the stupa was surrounded by an open area, where people would gather to pray for the welfare of Tibet and the people left behind. As time went on, ceremonial elaboration began to include the erection of prayer wheels: brass drums which spin on a well-oiled axis

Thangka painting of Kalachakra and lineage hanging in the temple at Norbulingka Institute.

containing large rolls of printed mantras and prayers, such as the name mantra of Guru Padmasambhava and the six-syllable mantra of Avalokiteshvara—the Bodhisattva of compassion, who is virtually the patron deity of Tibet. As people walk around the stupa, they spin the prayer wheels, turn a rosary in their hands, and recite prayers and mantras to themselves. This simple procedure involves the activities of body, speech and mind in spiritual practice.

A thangka being painted at the Norbulingka studio.

Norbulingka Institute

During the nineties, there has been a substantial increase in the number of Tibetans on the outskirts of Dharamsala. Down on the floor of the valley is the Norbulingka Institute, which is dedicated to the preservation of Tibetan art and culture. It is a large, beautiful place, whose buildings reflect the Tibetan style with broad walls richly decorated by the institute's own artists and which taper towards the top. The main complex has a unique ground plan laid out according to the shape of the deity of compassion, Avalokiteshvara, with eleven heads and a thousand arms.

Passing through the Institute's gateway, visitors are immediately impressed by the peaceful atmosphere of the lush green gardens. In this the

Mural paintings of Indian Buddhist geshis at the Norbulingka Institute.

Norbulingka Institute emulates the park of the same name near Lhasa that was the location of the Dalai Lama's summer palaces. The original Norbulingka was established by the seventh Dalai Lama in the 18th century to consolidate the artistic traditions of Tibet out of concern to preserve the quality of Tibetan art. The Norbulingka Institute aims to provide a supportive environment which emulates the guild system of artists and apprentices that existed in Tibet. Teams of artists are able to take on much grander commissions than an individual artist could; this gives the artists much greater scope and experience to develop their skills.

There are several workshops within the complex. One creates tents similar to those used in Lhasa for extensive picnics. In another, items from elaborate dolls houses to simple trays are decorated by hand. Another workshop preserves the traditional craft of making appliqué *thangkas*. This is painstaking work in which the piping is still made from horsehair and all the pieces are sewn together rather than glued. The huge *thangkas* made in this way are displayed during specific festivals. Several monasteries-in-exile have commissioned large *thangkas* here. The Institute also maintains a *thangka* painting studio (where you can observe artists of all levels of skill—from those who are just beginning to draw, to fully qualified master artists) besides wood carving and metal craft workshops.

The Institute's Academy of Tibetan Culture offers young people, who have completed their school education, the opportunity to train in higher

A colossal gilded copper statue of the Buddha that is the focus of the Seat of Happerim Temple at the Norbulingka Institute.

Facing page: Several monasteries have commissioned large thangkas *at the Norbulingka Institute.*

Many of the nuns at Dolma Ling had demonstrated against Chinese rule in Tibet and were consequently harshly treated. They arrived in India traumatised. At Dolma Ling they have found a degree of security once more.

Tibetan studies, in literary skills, such as poetics, history and philosophy. The aim is to train young people in the finer points of their own culture and enable them to express it in a global context.

A Literary and Cultural Research Centre employs a team of young researchers and writers, most of who were trained in Tibet, but who were unable to find any fruitful expression of their knowledge there because the Tibetan language is virtually suppressed in Tibet. This team of young writers puts together a monthly cultural newspaper in Tibetan, an annual journal of scholarly writing in Tibetan and a youth magazine. They are working to produce a Tibetan encyclopaedia in three volumes.

Togdem yogis from Tash'long, below Dharamsala in the Kangra Valley.

The Losel Dolls Museum houses a unique collection of nearly 150 exhibition dolls that depict the costumes of the different regions and various aspects of Tibetan society. They showcase how people actually used to dress in the local regions of Tibet before the Chinese takeover of the country. Great efforts have been made to ensure accuracy and that the materials are authentic. The dolls are made by a team of monks from the Drepung Loseling Monastery, which has been re-established in Karnataka, south India. The monks employ skills they already have: modelling, sewing and painting. Older Tibetans are often tearful at seeing things they had almost forgotten and children are awestruck at seeing things they have only heard about from their parents and grandparents.

The focus of the main Norbulingka complex is the Seat of Happiness Temple. The four traditional temple guardians, the guardians of the four directions, stand watch over the entrance. Once you step over the threshold of the brightly painted main doorway, you are immediately struck by the colossal statue of the traditional Buddha, Shakyamuni, which sits on a raised dais against the rear wall. This 14-feet, gilded copper statue was constructed within the temple itself by a team of statue makers, led by master Pemba Dorjee. He was also responsible for the statues in the Thekchen Chöling temple and is regarded as the only living master of this statue-making tradition in exile.

Work on this grand image took more than a year. The statue was fashioned from copper sheets, each piece being cut and worked on individually until it was ready to be gilded in a process using gold and mercury. The burnished parts were then assembled into the complete statue. During the assembly the statue was filled with precious and medicinal substances and collections of religious texts. Even the base was filled with various offerings, one level containing pieces of jewellery contributed by members of the Norbulingka community.

There are more than a thousand images in the murals lining the walls of the temple. Behind the Buddha statue a series of paintings depicts the twelve principal deeds of the Buddha's life from conception in his mother's

Left and facing page: Making stamped clay images of the deities of Long Life.

Pages 72-73: Tibetans nuns studying scriptural texts at Dolma Ling Nunnery.

womb, through his attaining enlightenment, to his passing away. Flanking them are paintings of the sixteen *arhats* who were the Buddha's principal disciples. Unique to this temple are a set of paintings of the fourteen Dalai Lamas around the upper balcony. The Great Fifth is on the eastern wall facing the Thirteenth and the Fourteenth Dalai Lamas, represented in actual likeness. Following the conventional pattern, the temple is crowned by an apartment for honoured guests, the most important of whom is His Holiness the Dalai Lama.

Dolma Ling Nunnery

Adjacent to the Norbulingka Institute is the Dolma Ling Nunnery which was established in the early 1990s to accommodate the great influx of nuns escaping from Tibet. Many of them had fled following their participation in demonstrations against the Chinese occupation of their homeland and their expulsion from their nunneries. Although many monasteries were re-established in exile, very few nuns arrived before 1991 so there were far fewer places where nuns could receive an education. At

Performers of the Tibetan
Institute of Performing Arts
off duty.

Dolma Ling, nuns are being trained in the Tibetan language and the scriptures and are engaged particularly in the philosophical practice of debate. Until this decade, there was no opportunity for nuns to engage in this traditional form of Buddhist education. While visiting Dolma Ling in the morning, one is likely to find the nuns in their classrooms, but in the afternoon, the courtyards come alive with clusters of nuns engaged in lively formal discussion of the topics they have been studying.

The Tibetan Institute of Performing Arts

The origins of the Tibetan Institute of Performing Arts (TIPA) go back to the early sixties, when the Tibetan Dance and Drama Society was founded in Kalimpong. The establishment of this institution is an indication that albeit very religious, preserving religion was not the only thing that concerned Tibetans. The performing arts, like so much else in Tibetan life, have strong religious associations, yet they reveal the lighter side of the culture. Tibetans are, in fact, quite happy to take things easy and enjoy themselves.

Shortly after the Dalai Lama settled in Dharamsala, TIPA was transferred here and has grown from strength to strength. It preserves the Lhamo opera, which began at the time of the great adept Tangthong Gyalpo, who travelled around 14th-15th-century Tibet improving communications by building bridges. His opera troupe came about when he gathered a group of girls to sing and dance for people in an attempt to raise funds for building a bridge. He trained them to perform so sweetly that people said that watching them was like being in the presence of goddesses or Lhamo. This is why the opera tradition is referred to today as Lhamo. Many of the performances tell stories based on Buddhist myths. Besides being entertaining there is always a moral to edify the audience.

TIPA maintains a wide range of associated traditions including singing and dancing, production and maintenance of the wonderful rich costumes and musical instruments. The Institute also trains people in the traditions of folk song and basic musicianship. Graduates go out into the Tibetan settlements in India and Nepal as teachers. Thus, there is a constant effort to keep these traditions alive. The Institute also provides specialist services, such as the formal welcoming ceremony when His Holiness the Dalai Lama is visiting or attending a particular function. During the Losar or Tibetan New Year celebrations, they are responsible for the court music at certain points in the proceedings and perform a special dance in the temple.

Performers of the Tibetan Institute of Performing Arts with their masks.

75

Tibetan Children's Village band leads proceedings on the Tibetan Uprising Day on 10th March.

Similarly, on occasions such as the Tibetan Uprising Day, 10th March, and His Holiness's birthday, 6th July, they lead the singing of the National Anthem. In Tibet a major opera festival called the Shotun or Yogurt Festival took place annually at the Norbulingka under the auspices of Drepung Monastery. TIPA today holds a Shotun festival early in the Tibetan new year, generally soon after the spring teachings that accompany the Great Prayer Festival.

The Tibetan Institute of Performing Arts provides training for musicians.

Facing page: A musician of the Tibetan Institute of Performing Arts, dressed in traditional costume, plays the phi-warg.

The Tibetan Children's Village

The first Tibetan Children's Village (TCV) was established very early on in 1960-61 at the present site above Tanglewood led by the first Principal, His Holiness's elder sister, Tsering Dolma. She created the pattern for subsequent TCVs. One of their most important functions was as an orphanage. Many of the children who, born in Tibet, had escaped into exile, were left bereft because their parents succumbed to the trauma of their escape, the rigours of the climate, and various diseases such as tuberculosis. Consequently, there were many orphans. TCV was set up as a group of family homes, each with house parents, who looked after the two-dozen or

Calisthenic performance during the anniversary celebrations of the Tibetan Children's Village (TCV).

so children living in their house. This provided them the opportunity of bringing up the children with Tibetan values and giving them some semblance of family life.

Many capable adults offered their services as teachers and, between them, they managed to set up a syllabus based on the Indian model, but tailored to suit Tibetan children with an emphasis on Tibetan studies. These were the circumstances under which the first generation of Tibetan children-in-exile, many of whom now hold responsible positions in the exile community, were educated.

Later, there were far fewer orphans. In the late seventies and early eighties, TCV became more like a boarding school for Tibetan refugee children. Then, in the mid-eighties, following a relaxation of restrictions in Tibet, there was a new influx of children from Tibet, seeking the education they were denied in their homeland.

For nearly 20 years there was very little communication between the community in Dharamsala and their families in Tibet. With the end of the cultural revolution, the easing of restrictions in Tibet and the opportunity for the government-in-exile to send in fact-finding missions, links were restored once more. Consequently, in the eighties, many Tibetan families brought their children out of Tibet to Dharamsala to ensure that they received a Tibetan education. This is still happening today.

Today, TCV provides opportunities for students to receive either an academic education or a vocational training according to their

A young artist from the Tibetan Institute of Performing Arts, waits to perform in the temple during Losar (New Year) celebrations.

Facing page, top: A flutist from the Tibetan Institute of Performing Arts plays at the Himalayan Festival.

Facing page, bottom: At the opera.

A young Tibetan Buddhist monk.

aptitude, but most of all, it inculcates in them a sense of their Tibetan identity. This is what makes it one of the major Tibetan institutions in Dharamsala.

Carpet Weaving

✠

One of the mainstays of the Tibetan economy is the production of carpets. There are several private and cooperative carpet-weaving enterprises in Dharamsala, as there are in many of the other settlements scattered through India and Nepal. They are quite different from the carpet factories that are the butt of criticism elsewhere, because the Tibetan carpet is thick and loosely knotted and is quite easily woven by adults sitting together at their looms in an enjoyable, friendly atmosphere.

Traditional carpets mostly consist of the 6-feet by 3-feet bed carpets, because in Tibet it is far too cold to sit on the bare ground. The point is not to carpet the floor, but to have a rug on the bed on which one can sit during the day and sleep at night. Here, in India, weavers have been able to expand their repertoire and produce carpets of a much greater variety. Another feature of Tibetan carpets is the clipping out of the pattern, which has an almost sculptural effect of enhancing the design. While women often do the weaving, men do the final clipping of the carpet. Nothing is wasted, because the clippings of wool are collected to make an excellent warm filling for cushions and mattresses.

Above and pages 88-89: Clipping out the pattern of a completed carpet in a carpet factory.

Facing page: Musical performance at the anniversary celebrations of the TCV.

Below: Dragon head water spout. Dragons are regarded as the protectors of the celestial realms. Dragon dribble is called norbu *(wish-fulfilling gem). Dragon bones are coveted by Tibetan doctors for their healing powers.*

Around Dharamsala

✠

There are several attractive places to walk to from McLeod Ganj and Dharamsala. One of the most charming is the spring and the temple of Bhagsunath. Legend has it that a king came here from Rajasthan in search of water for his drought-stricken people. He found water at this point and miraculously gathered it all into his bowl with the intention of taking it back to his suffering people. But he caught the attention of the powerful resident *naga,* the serpentine being who represented the spirit of the water source. Sorely displeased by the king's effrontery, it attacked and defeated him. The king pleaded that he had intended no harm and requested that at least his name should not be forgotten. Thus it was that the *naga* allowed King Bhagsu's name to be attached to his own, creating the name Bhagsunag or Bhagsunath.

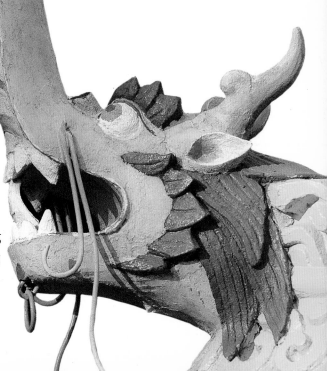

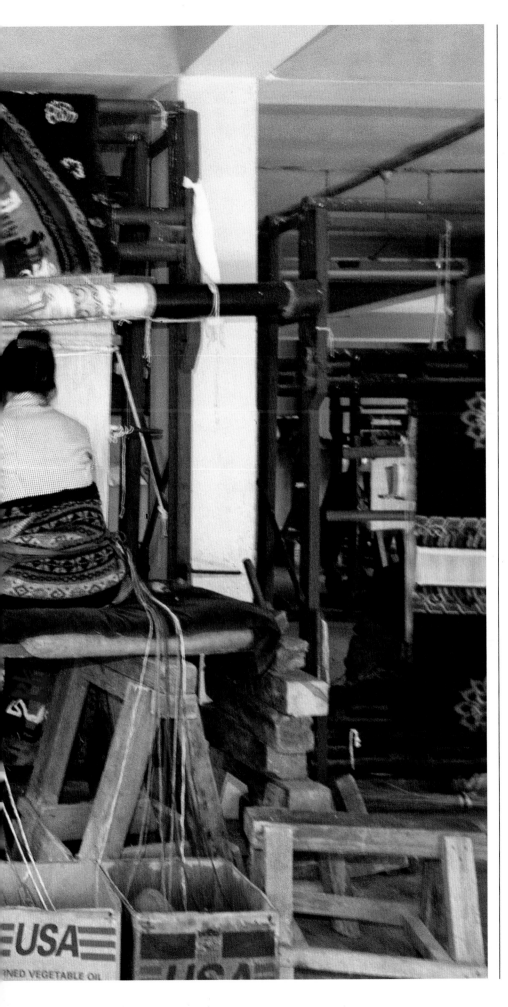

Working at the loom in a carpet factory at Dharamsala. There are several carpet-weaving factories in Dharamsala.

Many legends relate the power of this *naga*. Local people typically offer the first milk of their cow at the temple. It is said that in the course of a tussle, a king's bowl fell and some milk was spilt. A fresh-water spring came forth, which can now be seen flowing into the tank. Devout Hindus regard it as having sacred qualities and can be seen taking a holy dip in the water. Behind Bhagsunath a high waterfall pours into the Churan Khud, the thieving river which conceals its flow beneath its sandy bed except during the monsoon when it roars forth in a raging torrent. High above are the slate quarries which provide the high-quality tiles for local roofs.

A three-to-four-hour brisk walk out of McLeod Ganj brings you to Triond, a col at nearly 10,000 feet above sea level. From the verandah of the Forest Rest House can be seen picturesque views of the Kangra Valley down to the Pong Dam lake. There is also a precipitous path to the Indrahar pass, by which foolhardy trekkers and Gaddi shepherds cross the Dhauladhar mountains to reach Brahmour and Chamba beyond.

Every year on March 10, the anniversary of the Tibetan Uprising Day, Tibetans take out processions to demonstrate on behalf of Tibetan freedom.

The Mall Road leading out of McLeod Ganj towards TCV leads to the Dal Lake which is regarded locally as sacred. Its edge is dotted with small temples and its waters are populated by large somnolent carp. The road finally ends on the ridge of Talnu from where the most glorious views of the sunset can be seen. Descending from this point through wooded villages, a shepherd's track leads to the alpine lake of Kareri Dal and the Minkiani pass beyond it.

Beyond Kotwali bazaar, Dharamsala's main market, lie the pine-wooded slopes of the Chilgari estate, the location of the senior civil officers' residences. This gives way to one of the original British tea gardens which continues to be cultivated and produces the famous local Kangra tea. At the far edge of the garden stands the celebrated Kunal Patri temple, the focus of a local Spring fair.

The Kangra Art Museum on the edge of Kotwali Bazaar has a substantial permanent exhibition of Kangra miniature paintings. The last independent king of Kangra, Sansar Chand, was a leading patron of these paintings. These paintings are peculiar to the Himachal region and, following the style of Persian miniatures, represent one of the areas in which Hindu and Muslim traditions combined. In addition to Hindu religious themes, these paintings may depict the mood of a musical *raga*. The museum displays statues and other archaeological findings unearthed in the Kangra valley and also functions as a gallery for local contemporary artists.

The lower reaches of Dharamsala are home to the offices of the civil administration, the Forestry Department, the Police Station, the Main Post Office, the Zonal Hospital, the Medical College, the College and the Post Graduate College. A sombre war memorial commemorates those who died in the wars with China and Pakistan.

As part of the Tibetan struggle for freedom, there is a move to boycott Chinese goods.

Pages 94-95: Marching and chanting for Tibetan freedom.

The Future

Dharamsala has already gone through several incarnations. With its stunning scenery and comfortable climate, it will continue to attract people in search of respite from the heat and dust, the pollution, and the hustle and bustle of the cities of the plains. As for the Tibetans, His Holiness the Dalai Lama has, for forty years, spoken optimistically of returning to Tibet during his lifetime. He says: 'The return of freedom to our homeland is what so many Tibetans, men and women alike, have struggled for years in many different ways to achieve. I pray that as a culmination of all these efforts, our dream may soon be fulfilled.'

ISBN : 81-7436-086-7

© **Roli Books Pvt. Ltd., 2000**
Lustre Press Pvt. Ltd.
M-75, Greater Kailash-II Market
New Delhi-1100048, India
Tel: (011) 6442271, 6462782
Fax: (011) 6467185
E-mail: roli@vsnl.com
Web site: rolibooks.com

Foreword:
His Holiness the Dalai Lama

Text:
Jeremy Russell

Photo Credits:
Angus McDonald: 12-13, 18-19 (2 pix), 20, 23, 24, 25 (top),
43, 48, 49, 65, 80-81, 82 (top), 86, 87 (top), 88-89, 90-91
Diane Barker: 1, 2, 25 (bottom), 58
James Barllam Brown: 30-31 (3 pix), 66, 70, 71, 94-95
Rajiv Mehrotra: 32-33
Lustre Collection: 22, 34-35, 36-37, 38, 39, 40-41, 46-47,
52, 53, 54-55, 56-57, 59, 64, 67, 87 (bottom)
Thomas L. Kelly: 4-5, 10-11, 16-17, 21, 26 (top & bottom),
27 (top & bottom), 28-29, 41, 42, 44, 45, 50, 51, 55, 60, 61, 68, 69,
72-73, 74, 75, 76-77, 79, 82 (bottom), 83, 84-85, 92, 93
Tibet Image Bank:
Diana Barker: 6, 9, 14-15, 78, Edwin Maynard: 62-63

Printed and bound in Singapore